What If We All Bloomed?

Poems of Nature, Love, and Aging

What If We All Bloomed?

Poems of Nature, Love, and Aging

Poems by Victoria Doerper
Illustrations by John Doerper

Penchant Press International | Bellingham, WA.

Penchant Press International
PO Box 1333
Blaine, WA 98231
www.penchantpressinternational.com

Poems by Victoria Doerper 1949 -
Illustrations by John Doerper 1943 -
Cover Design by Spoken Designs www.spokendesigns.com
Author Photos by Rod del Pozo
Photo Designs by Robert Furlow

What If We All Bloomed? / Victoria Doerper. -- 1st Ed.
ISBN 978-0-9998048-1-0
LOCN 2019947961

Dedicated to my husband John,
who believed in my poetry
before I did.

Contents

What If We All Bloomed?

What if we all bloomed truth?
What if push and shove,
Take and conquer,
Those bitter forced fruits,
Blossomed instead
Into love?

What if we all bloomed
Unhampered by uncertainty,
Fortified by faith,
Tentative tendrils strengthened,
Vibrant blooms more vivid still,
Central songs unfurling
Into glitter and grit and balm?

What if we all bloomed
By embracing every tiny breath,
Every atom, every attempt
At growing into our full spirit
Together,
As in a garden?
But like no garden we've ever seen.

What if we all bloomed
Our very selves,
Together
In joint and several celebration,
Neither striving to be better
Nor fearing to be worse
Than each other?

What if we all bloomed
Our souls
In one grand community?
Would that be heaven?

Every Day A Song

If I fling seeds every day at dawn,
Will the words fly in to feed?
Will they scramble and scatter
And sort themselves in song?

If I pour out the pure nectar of thought
Will darts of emerald, humming words
Arc and dazzle in feathery display
To sip and shimmer like rocketing birds?

In spring if I wait by a hidden nest
Will I hear the cheeping of infant words?
Will I hear their first weak tottery notes
Transform to sure and steady singing?

At dusk, will the words fly home
After winging wild and wending long?
Will they gather with satisfied sighs
Where they belong?

Oh yes. Every day a song.

Frost's Secret *

On a fizzing bright spring day we
Sit outside. Our eyes dart as birds dance
Round neon green growth, round
The loose pink of purple plum in
Quickening blinks of wakening bloom. A
Giddy song of robin and wren will ring
Awake the slumbering coils of ferns and
Possibly alarm the worms, who I suppose
Are wiggling up a tender tip to test the air. But
Earth and sky can still surprise with storm. The
Trick for us in spring is "watch and wait." Her secret
Launches, totters, stalls, like baby jays. A parent sits
Nearby and screams encouragement, puts faith in
Flutters, fits and starts, falling and finding the
Way, past swagger of proud beginning, through middle
And muddle of storm and bleak uncertainty, and
Then—spring, a feathered sky, a heart that knows.

*A "golden shovel" poem structure,
inspired by Robert Frost's poem "The Secret."*

Aubade to Dawn

I'm addicted to the exotic crack
Of spring dawn possibility, to the hit
Of light in the first toke of smoky
Night giving way to the rosy glow
Of day. I'll cut sleep short to satisfy
My craving for the exquisite line
Of morning edging the far horizon,
And I'm dizzy for a first glimpse
Of new blooms in the awakening
Garden. My early a.m. thoughts
Intoxicate with heady promise
Of epiphany and poetic verve,
All perfect and lovely as gossamer
Wings of angels, surely hovering
On the shore, and in the yard,
Bestowing a vision of delights
Yet to come. And then the full
Blaze of sun moves in, beautiful
And compelling and heartbreaking.
Dawn dreams lift away
Like mist rises from a glassy pond.
The sun dares me to make a life
Still wonderful amidst daunting
Loss of perfect possibility.

Imperfect Beauty

Praise God for damaged things
Perfection trued by testing, try, and fail,
For raw red scaly scab of healing wounds,
For fallen soufflés, spilling paint, and tarnished rings,
For squeaking doors,
For starting boldly out then turning tail,
For bad directions, wilted flowers, and ragged plumes,
For broken plates that resurrect on bright mosaic wings,
For mismatched mates and misdirected mail,
For bulbs of scarlet tulips, rising in a golden bloom,
For spackled spark of beauty in tender broken things,
Praise God for this, most unexpected boon.

Eating the Light

I want to eat the light
Like a tree does,
Taking in little bites
Of the luscious sun.

I want to sop up
The thick gravy of soil,
Rich with drippings
That will fatten my soul.

I long to savor the rain,
Imbibe its heady spirit,
And feel its fizz run
Up and down my frame.

And who wouldn't want
To sip up the wind
Through tiny leafy straws,
Noisily sucking it in.

I want the deer to browse,
Not too greedily,
On my filigree of juicy green,
And tickle me with their nibbling lips.

I want to sway in a wild dance
With light and wind, soil and rain,
Until I'm left gasping for breath
And exhaling blossoms.

And in the dark season
I ask for just a few pale morsels
Of sun, to curb my keening hunger,
To soothe me until the light returns.

Stars

If I could pluck
From the distant midnight sky
A fistful of celestial roots,
I'd shake off the damp moonlight
And grate their tough tops
To make a thick paste
Of white-hot Wasabi stars,
Then take a tiny taste
And wait for the rush of sparks
To burn my throat, like a first breath
Of freezing air on a clear night
So pure and cleansing it hurts.
Or I would pick the dangling fruits
Hanging on heaven's ancient vine
And crush them into juice,
Then feel the tang of sparkle
Prickle over my placid tongue
Like vintage bubbly.
With a proof of some ten billion
That would rouse up quite a buzz.
Or I could draw together all the strands
Of each bright silver constellation
And weave a prayer shawl of light
To drape around the sagging shoulders
Of all the hurt and sorrowing in the universe,
Or soften the stars into an astral poultice
To heal every single wound in the world.
And then I'd take a handful of star-seeds
And scatter them in our front garden,
Where they would spray out sparks
Of flowery blessings to perfume the dark air.

Their fruits would ripen into glittering orbs
Of once-forsaken dreams.
I'd gather them up then,
In bags and baskets and backpacks,
And wander the neighborhood,
Delivering them into tired and aching hands,
Holding back just one for me,
To eat in the garden,
Standing there with a giddy smile
And dripping starlight down my chin.

Tending Trees

The thread of mortality
Spools and spins long
For women who live
Among trees,
In the close press of kin,
Breath to breath, skin to skin,
Bloom to breast, bark to palm,
Eye to branch, arm to limb,
Pine, cedar, yew, plum,
Our bones and blood,
Trunks and buds,
Flowering into one another,
Pulsing numinous with light,
Beaming, glowing, flickering,
Growing older than time can count
In our leafed love.

How to Range Rove

Take nothing shiny with you,
No waxed gleam, no metal sheen,
No glint and sparkle of slick glass.
Let a creek scrambling over stones
Break the wild sunlight and scatter
Shining fragments like living things
To rise up in a shimmer of greeting.
You may, however, take the glimmer
Of your wide open eyes with you.

Take nothing rumbling or thrumming,
No thundering super-charged engine
Propelling your progress over the range.
Let the staccato thud of woodpecker
Hammering against thick tree trunk
Quicken your step and fill your ear.
You may, however, take the thumping
Of your excited wild heart with you.

Take no fossil-fueled oil-burning exhaust,
No fumes of spectral sparks and fires,
No hot vapors to confuse the free air.
Let the must of wet soil and honey of clover
Surround you in a wide and open embrace,
Unimpeded by the mask of sputtering gas.
You may, however, take the fire and spark
Of your super-charged imagination with you.

Let your eye range and your body rove
Free of manufactured clattering contraption.
Glide in with the wind, like a migrating bird.
Feel the air feathering your hair, filling your lungs,
The strange scent of a home you once knew.

Hedgerows

I'm convinced that heaven
Lurks in old hedgerows,
Not like a predator, but
More like a mystery
Laced through thickets
Tangled with song,
In those byzantine temples
Of leafy, shaggy, profligate
Bud, flower, and berried
Commonplace delight,
Visited by visions of roses
Wafting the incense of attar
Into the sacred air,
Where angels shelter
The hungry, the trod-upon,
The sky-travelers seeking rest,
No questions asked,
No proof of worthiness,
No papers required
For an offer of ground
In an unsullied place
Filled with the potent
Possibility of grace.

I Secretly Smile at Dogs

I secretly smile at dogs. I also subtly wave
Or surreptitiously waggle my hand as I walk by.
I salute from sidewalks and from inside my car.
Dogs barking behind windows get a friendly nod,
And wriggling puppies can't be more excited than I
When they rush at me with clumsy limbs
And enthusiastic faith in kindness,
A faith I wish I still had. I admire the spirits of dogs,
And they seem to know it. We make eye contact
As between peers, neither of us needing to settle
Questions of dominion or opinion or status or worth.
We covertly flirt in the presence of their owners,
On streets or in dog parks or crowded parking lots.
And even though I know their predatory instincts,
Propensity for rolling in rotting, stinking, stuff,
Sniffing butts and eating the most disgusting things,
I look into their eyes and see a deep veracious spark
That flames up in joy with small, repetitive, daily actions,
And I long to be glad as those ball-chasing
Frisbee-leaping tail-spinning scrabbling barking
Laser focused in-the-moment
Inhabitants of canine Canaan.
So I secretly smile at dogs.
They almost always smile back.

Trail Music

The note rises like a startled heron,
Sudden sound leaping up, then swooping,
Lifting again and gliding high, circling
Spirals that shiver the very air
Into something like hammered gold.
I'm walking my daily route between
Grey concrete of the treatment plant
And the tall, gangly stand of trees
Holding a small village of herons
Nesting. But this sound isn't the squawk
Of great blues in raucous tête-à-tête.
I walk on, wondering if some varied thrush
Is trilling out a silvery lovesick sonata,
Or if a lovestruck loon is calling to his lady.
I round the bend and before the lagoon
I see a quick flash of flute
In the warm brown hands of a man in a cap,
Face toward the water, fingering with care
A melody for no one but the open air,
The woods, the marshy shore,
Wild roses, blackberries, buffleheads,
Flowering currant, mallards, deer.
The flute player doesn't see me
Amidst wings, petals, wind, bramble, grass—
Camouflage for my quiet astonishment.

Spreckled Spring

Spreckly comes the greengilled spring
Flecketing freshness over everything,
Warblitting in floaty tunes and flight,
Shallishoaling darkness into light,
Rapplewamps the calcatating weather,
Silkisashes every flower and feather,
Rallifluffles each and every wan and ragged thing,
Spreckly, spreckly comes the greengilled spring.

A Slander of Slugs

A slander of slugs
Pretends to be
Harmless in bland ubiquity,
And slow scrawls on the ground.

These scattered commas punctuate
In slimy misplaced unctuate,
Ingest and thus obliterate
Pristine leaves by the pound.

Aspersions cast in trails of slime
Besmirch our garden's coming prime,
Become a gnawing damn vexation
Blast our garden's reputation.

Yet we are on the side of right
And so with coffee grounds invite
Our sluggy armies to decamp
Into a different burgeoning damp.

Who holds the key
To calumny
Must yield apace
To truth's good grace.

Fish Pond

Down the hill, the ragged thorny green
Of the blackberry-leaping land
Takes custody of the old pond
And its viscous flits of shimmery fish
That lip up specks of larvae
Left by gadabout mosquitoes
On this quiet circle of water,
This silver skim and swish of gold,
Sure as a dream, fluid as vision,
The place where solid and liquid
Hold each other in a fine moment.
The water below, the billow of sky,
The graze of swaying fish
Old as prehistory.
I think those fish
Catch the fleeting shape
Of the world's mystery
Through the wide open
Lens of water-wet eyes,
Through the relentless
Filter of scale-glazed gills,
While I sit on the bank
And can barely catch
My breath.

Great Blue

Fish eater, water-stalker,
Killer of moles and muskrats,
Eater of roots,
Feathered squawker, flapper of blue-grey
Silklet strands, curved head plumes,
Neck like a snake,
Flies up before me like a first kiss—
Compelling urge upwells to awkwardness,
Slipping to a sweet, soft gliding grace—
Wings touch the clouds, then dip away
To the clay-blue bowl of the lake.

Might I Recommend Quiet?

Might I recommend
Staying quiet for a day,
Or if you cannot manage that,
An hour. For the recalcitrant,
Try counting to a hundred, silently,
And let your thoughts settle,
Let them rest in the beaded reticule
Of your beautiful, still-life brain,
For just a while.

Give the world a quiet space
To work some magic.
Leave off noisily kneading thick thought,
Let the yeasty blossom of airy light
Leaven in rest and solitude.
Do not insult your soul
By filling your mind's bowl
With a dense dumb dough
That gives no rise at all.

While your resolve still holds,
Silence electronic chatter;
Don't panic, let that low crackle
Flow and foam around you;
You, a venerable boulder
In a river of rush and swirl.

Let the hush
Of muscles twitching slow,
Buds on verge of break,
Rising yolk tapping shell,
Quell the din of loathsome bullies.

Be the mute little monkey
Of the organ grinder,
Your quiet outstretched hand
Grateful to clasp offerings
From unknown fingers
While gaudy clang grinds the air around you.

Go to the still shore of waiting.
Sit quiet. The steady flow of waves
Will keep you company, present odd gifts
On the flow, leave them at your feet on ebb.
You will gather them in.
Bits of shimmery shell still salt-sea clammy,
Surf-weathered wood, a dented beer can.
They will know your name.

And after quiet for a time,
A moment more than comfort begs,
Spring out splashing wild
From the deep center of yourself,
Thundering in all foamy iridescence
With wild and rolling combers in your hair,
Your head thrown back in throaty singing,
Breaking in spumy music on the shore.
Your mustang-mind running now,
Tawny mane flying,
Hoofs pounding energy,
Sparking up the fire of lips
And kiss and tangle of loins,
Of heart beating fast.

Perhaps I might,
Once again—
While I have your attention—
Recommend quiet.

Wild Water

Water rockets
Left and right
Round boulders
Tight pressed
In pockets of cliff
Then falls heedless
In spume and thunder
Pounding down
Surging under
Broken limbs
Bounding up
Flowing on again
Strong as a silver
Scour of gravel
Silt sculpting rock
Building up a mantle
Of remembrance
In deposits along
The further banks,
Signs that once
Water had a wild
Encounter
With constraint
But left behind
Less than what
She kept
And carried
Forward.

Cow and Ganges

She wanders along, brown and bony,
Clops down wide stone steps,
Stops and pauses above the sand
Sweeping the shore of the holy Ganges.
A sacred symbol of motherhood
And all encompassing care,
She wears the present and future
Fate of the world on her bones.
Standing there alone, she seems to scan
The dark river wistfully, perhaps wishing
She could plunge in and wash away
This heavy burden of divinity.

Beads of Blessing

I keep a strand of dove grey porcelain beads
My husband gave to me some years ago
In easy reach on the shelf behind the bed
For nights that toss the coverlet and pillow
Into storming disarray; I'll fumble for my beads,
Once prayed over by a hundred hushed voices
Whispering to God for comfort and release
From suffering, and transmutation of grief.
A quiet, centered breath infuses each
Small sphere as it rests in tender palms.
I imagine holy hands holding smooth beads
Joined together by the plumb line of a quiet song,
Of closed eyes and the calm of willing heart
Conveying broken blessings sprung from pain
Made whole again in sacrament of offering
To bless another.

Muck

I once saw a lumpy tumble of peat moss
Curdling a swampy pond littered with leaves,
Churning and bubbly and awash in stink.
The muck almost drove me away.
But not quite. I made myself look down,
Breathe in that thick, strong, fecund,
Overpowering smell of dirt and detritus,
Transforming.
Maybe this is what the odor of sanctity
Turns out to be. Not the scent of roses,
But ferment of the fallen still striving.

Henry Vaughan Responds at 3 A.M.

Blanket-tangled, I thrash with nightmares—
My husband is falling... and falling ... and falling.
Floods buck and surge, and I am swept away,
A flailing figure sinking in a meaningless sea.
I jerk awake. Then my conscious mind
Takes over, conjures scenes of North Korea
Sending bombs to our coast, cratering the shore,
Rubbling the streets. But civil war may flare
Before that happens. Those are the "maybes."
The sure things are aging, disability, death.
What's the point?
My overactive worry-squad has no answer.
Finally I switch on my bedside lamp
And fumble on the floor for my book—
Anthology of Poetry in English.

The pages flop open to the seventeenth century
And Henry Vaughan, Welsh poet and physician,
Appears before me, heroically making
An emergency middle-of-the-night house call.
He's traveled well over three hundred and fifty years
To be here with me on this rest-less dark night,
To resuscitate my faith in something
Beyond nihilism and entropy.
Henry just saw eternity the other night:
"A great ring of pure and endless light," he says.
He throws it to me like a life ring
And I grab on tight. He hauls me up
Into the safety of the hard-backed boat
That is this buoyant book of poetry,
Crowded with dozens of first responders—

Wordsworth, Dickinson, Frost, Keats, Levertov,
Breathing out beauty and truth in calm rhythm
Onto page after page of this musty volume
That I bought in college,
Long before I ever knew
How many times and ways
I would need saving.

Buddha Belly

An old man's belly
Swells the spinnaker
Of his white T-shirt
Into a parabolic curve.
He rests still and quiet
With an almost smile on his face,
Sitting in a lawn-green folding chair
Under a tree in the park by the sea.
He reads and reads, pages swishing,
Not heeding the kids playing,
Not the kayakers,
Not the wedding parties,
Not the scolding crows,
Not the radios of the gardeners,
And, presumably, not the worries
Of the reeling, reckless world
That I walk.

I see him in the park every day,
A solitary, self-contained party of one,
Center of some serene universe
Far beyond my ken.
I always wonder
Whether I could manage to nip in
And swipe a soft circular rub
On that beckoning Buddha belly,
Snatch up some scrap of serenity
Before he could notice that I,
Worry-wracked aerobic walker,
Had dared to touch him,
Had possibly caused some virtue

To go out from him.
But maybe, just maybe, he would
Calmly look up from his serene world,
Unsurprised by my audacity and my need,
Look straight and honest into my eyes,
And I would go in peace.

Coast

Surely a magician conjured up
The wild passion of a brimming coast
Spread to splash, churn, and flow
Under a tent of star-spattered sky,
Performing marvels and exotic acts
For our very own amazement.

Consider the seabed's scandalous tabloid,
Featuring soft bodies and hard shells,
Teeming with drama.
Then ponder the contents of a tidepool
Pulsing with a retinue of tiny jeweled beasties
Beat down upon by a brazen sun,
And rescued just in time by a raucous spill of waves.

Glide like a shearwater
Over a swirling pageant
Of orange and teal anemone ballet.
Sidle up to sea stars or swim
With a dazzling dash of parrot fish,
Then hang with limpets on a rock mosaic,
Or with the wild and grasping mollusk crowd.

Let this flagrantly grand display
Push your own grinding routines
Into redeeming disarray,
Plunge your tired linear brain
Into scrolls of curling foam,
And free yourself from the tether
Of habit. Focus your mind here,
On this beautiful ragged edge,
This disappearing world.

A Lamentation Terzanelle

Carolina parakeets have tumbled out of days
Wild pigeons fall like darkness from the skies.
In ignorant worlds, no species ever stays.

The golden toad, now lost, has no bright eyes
To sweep the gathered green of pond and leaf,
Wild pigeons fall like darkness from the skies.

Regret for damage done brings no relief,
Our lots and timbered lands are cut by blades
To sweep the gathered green of pond and leaf.

The names of things forever lost line up in sad parade.
Soft fur of pygmy rabbit gone, Vancouver wolverine,
Our lots and timbered lands are cut by blades.

Fashion's slaughter. Feathered hats. But no birds preen.
Ivory-billeds and great auks drop from view.
Soft fur of pygmy rabbit gone, Vancouver wolverine.

Carolina parakeets have tumbled out of days,
Rhinoceros and amber heath hens too.
The burdened, weary sentinels can only toil and pray.
In ignorant worlds, no species ever stays.

The Last Era

In the morning light
A wind riffles the sea
And seems to reveal
A curve of something
Solid, like the back
Of a whale, but not
A whale. Some think
It's a trick of light,
Or a glimpse of
The mythic island.
It's a mystery,
But the people tell stories.
Some say that long ago
Golden, grasping creatures,
Who believed themselves
Gods lived here. Others
Believe that a fabled land
Deep beneath the waves
Holds secrets and treasure.
The old patriarchs maintain
There never was anything
Except this endless water.

Pieces of Earth

Someone is always claiming
Pieces of earth, pushing the
People and boundaries of history
And family, geology and biology,
Punching and exploiting or
Fracking, hacking, and sucking
Something precious from deep
And slumbering pools of time
As if this time, our time, is all
There is to matter. The trees
Know better, and we should too,
Such a simple lesson from the earth
That gardens learn and recite back
In creamy blossom of pear, carmine
Camellia petals, withies of willow
And curving twine of lowly grape,
Rising above boundary lines
And blood feuds and ideology.
How witless we can be, and how wise
We might become if we tended to each
Other's gardens.

How to Climb Out of a Hole

There you are,
Your neck craned back
Looking up at the far stars
From the wrong end
Of a telescope,
Everything
Distant and dark.

First, sit still, and feel
The suffocating fog
Of gloom drop over you,
A leaden pool of regret,
Or disbelief, or endless
Sadness. Let it seep
Under your dreams.

When you're done with that,
Let one sting of desire
Move you to curse for awhile.
Feel the vibration of your anger
Thrum through your bones
Like fire.

Then take the kindest words
You've ever heard spoken,
The ones that glow
With empathy and love,
And mix them with
The most honest kicks
In the ass you've ever had.

Heap up the stones
That are strewn about.
Balance them into cairns
Of comfort and direction.
Look around, your eyes have
Grown accustomed to the dark.

Take the hands
Outstretched to help you,
Even if they are only your own.

How to Receive Songs of the Little Birds

Open your window just a slot. Waves of air
Waft in, unspooling ribbons of sound
Abundant as the silks of Samarkand,
In smooth taffeta trills, cheeps of hot pink,
Plangent orange, all floating through air,
Spirited and swirling in canals of your ears,
Plucking the thinner-than-thinnest
Silken thread-like cells, making them hum
In robin, towhee, sparrow, siskin, junco, wren.
Some songs you've forgotten,
Some you don't know yet.
Close your eyes and let the waves carry you.
Receive them, the songs of the little birds.
Let them melt into you,
Little wafers at the edge of your tongue.

Garden Love

A carnival of fecund lovers
Floats, struts, and sashays,
Flirts, flaps, swoops, and sways
In rituals of wild seduction.

Chorus lines of blousy blooms
Spring up from unkempt beds
And tilt coquettish heads
At wandering swarms
Of buzzing lovestruck bees,
As dainty painted ladies
Tipple and tickle
Their milkweed swains,
And woodpeckers drum
A hollow-tree love song.
Acrobatic acts ensue,
As squirrels trapeze through trees,
The males in ardent search
Of lively girls with fluffy tails
Who will—for once—hold still.

Hummingbirds then magically
Appear at center stage,
Where a sun-soaked male soars
Higher and ever higher skyward,
Then dives, down and down and down,
With blazing feathers vibrating fast
As a stringed instrument of romance,
Wooing a winsome clique of females far below,
While a calliope of sparrow tongues flings out
Brash tunes into the dappled canopy,

And the two of us, bedazzled spectators,
Sit on the steps of our sturdy old porch,
Shoulder to shoulder, holding hands.

Campfire

As embers cool,
We match kiss for
Kiss, light for light,
Sparking this deep
Mid-summer's night
With a flicker of new flame.
Our surprised eyes
Reflect in the stars,
Our souls tune
To prehistoric light.

Yellow Wings Triolet

I hum in yellow wings, I whir in green,
I agitate the air with hot pink singing,
I stroke your limbs, your lips, your hair, and in between
I hum in yellow wings, I whir in green.
I smooth your face, caress your hands, and paint a dream
Onto midnight skin. We come together like a bell ringing.
I hum in yellow wings, I whir in green,
I agitate the air with hot pink singing.

Ghazal of Love

The sun shines upon my face and warms me forever,
Love flows and lingers here in waters of forever.

Your kiss of sweet plumeria scents my whole world,
Your frangipani embrace whispers of forever.

Inhale and exhale, our breathing thunders and rushes,
The surge of our love foams in a sea of forever.

Our leaves grow side by side, vines twine about each other,
Our roots plunge deep, piercing the bedrock of forever.

The sun makes bright images, the moon makes a path.
We follow the moon to the garden of forever.

Cowboy Kiss

My sweet sixteen was coming
And I'd never had a kiss
Except from relatives and dogs
And once a neighbor kid
Who did it on a dare. So there
One starry night in June
I came back from a ride
Wondering whether some time soon
I'd have a kiss, not just a peck,
Cause what the heck,
My birthday wasn't far away
And how could I endure sixteen
Without a grownup kiss.
And there was Vince, the stable hand,
With lips so full and hips so slim,
His Levi's sang a sexy song,
Even his belt was in love with him,
And so was I. And so was
Every other girl who had a horse
At the Circle Bar. That night
He lightly brushed my hand,
Taking the halter rope from me,
Since it was dark he said
He'd better keep me company
Back to my horse's stall. So there
We were behind the barn
The smell of horse and hay
And sweat and dust, and then
He kissed me, deep and sweet,
Under the star-filled sky.
I thought, right there, I might just die

Of pleasure and relief.
A handsome cowboy kissed me
Before I turned sixteen.

A Blessing for Cantankerous Couples

May your rants and your raves
Be as rain in the trees,
May the curses you spit
Fall like dew on the leaves,
May your strident complaining
Dissolve into doves,
May the dawn find you smiling
Astonished by love.

Two Trees

Next to the gravel driveway
A cedar and Douglas fir
Press trunks in close embrace.
They've leaned so long together
It's hard to tell whose limbs are whose,
Which one is holding up the other.

Old Wine, for My Husband

A young grinning Beaujolais
Splatters insouciance
On new lovers in new skins,
Fans up the fleet sparks of youth
For awhile. But we demur
The mad dash for that fresh girl.
We, old lovers in old skins,
Don't mind waiting for the fire.
Rough tannins tumble smooth,
Raw lust sculpted into strong
Chiseled angles of desire,
The genre poetry, not news,
Stays true beyond the first
Season. We will reach the last
Vintage one of these days,
And pour what's left of ourselves
In silky sigh of transmuted fruit
Like a spill of seasoned Cabernet,
Clear ruby sparkle, grape spent,
Bottle empty, lees left behind.

Index of Love

Our love beats
The market
Every single time,
Rising and falling
Like stocks do,
Hyped by expectation,
Pressed down by a cloud.
We have no strategy
For buy and hold,
Yet we hang on
Through Black Fridays,
Sudden panics,
And when the bears
Start roaring,
We grip each other tight,
Your hand and mine
As compelling as
The closing bell
On a good day,
A plot point on
The index of love.
An unbroken line
Traces our shape—
Trough, crest, curve,
Sky, beach, sea:
We spiral
Into infinite gold.

Mid-July

I wake and rise
To perpetual blur of blue
Days in a summer run
Of soft-yolked mornings
So thick I mop them up
With buttered toast,
This jay-cracked dawn
Of mid-July, pried open
By the season's turn of sun.

Perhaps the sun will stay
To baste the droop of spirits
Bent with strain and care
Of sadness, old grief, despair,
Human depths to which
Wild creatures seldom fall.
Perhaps the willowy light
So lithe, so flush with balm
Will make us strong.

Perhaps the sun will make
A scattered seedbed bake
Into a flowering tiramisu
Laced with cream and blush,
While the mild blue sky
Looks on in approbation.
Perhaps the fragrant scent
Of one new honeysuckle bud
Will make us glad.

Perhaps the waning dusk-bound sun
Will melt the buttery yellow rays
To sugar pink, soft lilac, brilliant red
Streaking the background blue
To a brindled, breathless blaze
Flashing from the sky's last glance
Before light goes dark, before time turns.
Perhaps the luminous afterglow
Will make us bold.

Perhaps a night-calmed summer sun
Will wake again in perfect yeasty bloom
From darkly quiet rest, and leap into
Perpetual leavening of life's new dough
From now to the next and the next and the next day,
Kneaded by the push of strong and faithful
Palms, fists, and smooth knuckles of God.
Perhaps the rising up of this one day in mid-July
Will make us wise.

Fragments

An air of smoky mystery swirls around the half-done,
The fragments, the abandoned, the once-begun,
The house half built, the painting sketched out,
Struggling words stranded like whales on a beach,
A song stumbling, then falling mid-way to silence.
Someone, maybe you, started something, then failed
To conclude; began, then left some bits behind
For the great, swarming, fertile, flailing universe
Of other people, including us, to interpret,
As we always do, with a question, or a judgment,
Gratitude, or regret for what could have been.
The earth thrums under our feet in a quaking rumble
Of grand beginnings, discontinued dreams, wild gestures
Of human striving, quiet maundering on after truths,
Darting thoughts that give us a shiver of recognition, then
Disappear, a chimera in the mirror, the big one
That got away. We leave our trembling undone,
Little vulnerable fragments. We leave them as gifts,
Or curses, or messages in a bottle,
Genies in an unrubbed lamp,
For those who come after.

Revelation

I keep an empty can of Revelation
On my window sill, plucked years ago
From detritus left in my father's garage
After he died. Amongst a jumble
Of sandpaper, hammers, wrenches,
Saw blades and dry cell batteries,
I saw a dim glow of black, red, cream,
The tin where Dad's tobacco once lived.
Into that then-pristine can his pipe bowl
Dipped, dug, swirled, extracted.
Then he tamped and touched with flame,
Breathed in. The smoke of sweet leaves
Drifted up and over my head like a prayer.
The battered can I found in the garage
Held handfuls of washers, nails, screws
That rattled around like dry bones
In the desert, as if my memories
Could prophesy Dad back to life.
But I'm no prophet. What could I do
But empty the can, take it home,
And breathe in every now and then
The sweet scent of Revelation.

Doors of the Moon

The moon holds the key
To twelve doors.
Imagine them opening
One after the other.
Exit one room,
Enter another,
Proceed through
A calendar of colors,
Mellow gold, neon green,
Cold bright white,
Faded darkness.
The moon unlocks
Each month's door,
Hinged on an axis of time,
Nudges us into rooms
We seem to remember
From twelve months,
Or countless years before.
I always loved best
The golden rooms,
Filled with long sunshine,
And warm breezes,
Except one August afternoon
When the impatient moon
Grasped my hands,
Still clutching at the doorjamb,
And sent me staggering
Into the next room,
Locking my mother out.
In the cruelest months
The moon throws away
The key.

Eclipse

I lost the moon today.
I thought she would stay
Forever, but in the dark
Of very early morning,
She slipped away,
Beneath a shadow
So gradual, it was like
The melting of glaciers.

Wu Tong Triolet

I sip on lukewarm coffee.
The sky outside is flat grey.
The Wu Tong has no flowers for me.
I sip on lukewarm coffee,
Remembering purple blooms swelling the tree
When everything was different than today.
I sip on lukewarm coffee.
The sky outside is flat grey.

Twenty-Four Ladybugs

I found twenty-four ladybugs today,
Scattered over the floor and
On up the stairs, as if they were
Searching for some way out,
As if they didn't know how they'd got in.
They looked perfect in their shiny
Scarlet and polka-dotted black,
Quiet, as if they were resting,
But they were all dead.
I stooped and picked each one up,
One by one by one,
Let them rest in the center of my hand,
Then laid them out with tenderness
On the lawn. Too late, but a last dignity,
A last honor, compassion for their last act,
Because who among us has not wandered
And gotten lost and climbed those stairs,
Searching for something that we never found.

My Husband's Map

I see South America swelling
On my husband's right thigh,
A ragged continent in mottled ebony
With a wide swath etched in red
And scratched across Brazil.
Like some reluctant Columbus
Or Vasco da Gama,
He's pushed off for a journey
Into the unknown.
He's already discovered
His own volcano, a fiery lava-
Spewing crater situated
On the ball of his right foot.
And now his chronometer
Stutters and slips, and the sky
Is cloudy most of the time,
So he's navigating blind.
His body is our new map
We finger like braille,
Hoping to come upon currents
That keep us on course,
That keep us from falling
Off the edge of the world.

Translating Your Eyes

A foreign language sleeps
Beneath the fringe of your lashes,
Amidst the flecks of amber in your
Hazel eyes, and if I could dive
Through the dark guarded portals
To the deep cavern of your soul
I might discover secrets there,
The hieroglyphics of your life
Etched in tissue and bone.
Decades of deciphering
Your outward omens and signs
Might prepare me to decode
The unexplored meanings inside,
To find the hidden stories
Even you don't know.
I might be able to translate
And make a poem for you.
Then we might both understand.

Flame Test

When you had a body full of purpose,
And not a body full of perdurable pain,
I stood in awe of your pure and brilliant hues.
I imagined a flame test of your elemental metal,
With you spurting up high in carmine passion,
Shining bright in salty yellow-gold,
Glowing fierce with fiery blue-white force.
But that was yesterday, and yesterday, and yesterday.
Now when I dredge my imaginary platinum loop
Through the powder of your body's box of pain,
Your flame test wavers in unfamiliar dimness.
I watch that little flicker of your beautiful being,
Colors faded into a washed-out pale pastel,
And I wonder what I should do.
If I pounded out a piece of myself,
Sprinkled it over your ground-down pain,
Could we raise a new flame together,
Spark the scarlet that flares
From sacrificial cochineal?

Tulips

We stayed away from the tulip fields this year.
When my husband was well, we'd drive
In quadrangles, rectangles and squares,
Tracing geometric shapes on the land,
With solid blazing colors shimmering
In such brilliance that the earth warmed us.
Now I bring tulips inside, trim their stems,
Plunge the severed ends into water.
Vases substitute for the good, rich,
Dark earth of fields.
The stems crowd down into a cylinder.
Up top, the tulips lean out and away,
Making the shape of a wide open fan.
Pink, red, orange, purple, streaky colors
Glow in a smoky sunset.

Emergency Rations

Who knows how many
Years are left?
With my birthday
Numbers mounting,
I've slipped
Into a new routine,
Collecting bits
Of past days
And daubing them
Onto pages.
The feathers,
Bright shells,
The ropey tangles
Of indecision,
All the shards
Of broken things,
The threads of delight
That hold everything
Together.
I tuck all those pages
Away on a back shelf,
Emergency rations
For those I love
When I finally
Have to leave them.

Saint Sane

In breathless rush
Of wrestling
With a problem
Or a person
Or a heartbreak
Of tangled humanity
Suffering in a wilderness
Of pain
I conjure up Saint Sane,
Wearing a jaunty beret
And a string of bright orange
Beads that pop.
In one hand is a stick
She uses to walk
Difficult terrain;
The other hand is free
To gesture and proclaim
The oddest beauty
Of the moment,
And pin it, perhaps,
Like a sparkling brooch
To a sagging shoulder.

If Saint Sane
Were in my shoes
She would raise up
Her hem to better tap
A staccato dance,
Or toss her percussives
Altogether
And glide

Softly barefoot,
Feeling the warm sweep
Of golden sand
Anointing her feet.

But I am not
Saint Sane
So I churn and tremble
At odd moments,
Missing the beauty
Yet hoping still to find
Some spark of joy
Near the dark center.

The Old Women

They join together,
Like late season apples,
Fragrant beneath crinkly skins,
Full of mellow sweetness,
Though tart and tangy too,
Bubbling hot and juicy
Under a cobbler-crumbled crust.

They sound in clear notes of silver
Bells, the trickle of autumn waters
Kissing each stone, caressing each pebble,
Singing music into the gathering silt.

They are old, these women who gather
Beads, buttons, threads, and shells,
Who patch badges onto tattered sashes
Draping their singular, well-worn cloth.

They weather like ancient wood,
With seasons rooted in their cells,
Remnants of storm, drought, and sun,
Of wind or lick of fire or slash of ax.

Stories bloom in their gnarled gardens,
Heartwood old and just unfurled,
Wildflower rangy and stoic as stone,
Shining brilliant as the leaves fall.

Hand to the plough, they once again till
The old soil faithfully, turning and tending,
Watering, watching, awaiting
Some unknown harvest yet to come,
Trusting now in the vagaries of weather,
Each other, and the seeds they scatter.

Hands

My hands were smooth and beautiful once.
Now blue-green veins swell
Like pipelines traversing skin,
And splotches of burnt umber
Hover over a delta of bones,
Shading the infinities of sunlight.
Bruises bloom with the least little nudge,
And rings no longer fit,
As if my finger bones were trees
Adding rings to their heartwood,
Thickening with each season.
My niece asks, "What's wrong
With your hands?" As I look down
She traces snaky rivers
With smooth ten-year-old fingers.
"Nothing's wrong," I say,
"They just got old."
"When?" she asks, and I wonder
How to tell her that years slide by
Unnoticed by the days, while we're wielding
A pencil or tray, a scalpel or carrot stick,
Pattering over keys of piano or laptop,
Cleaning up dishes or arguments
Or sheets after hot nights of surprising love,
Tickling giggling children and soothing
Hot foreheads on endless nights of flu.
How to explain hands that have petted
Seven generations of dogs, fed more
Birds than can be counted,
Comforted babies and friends,
Held trembling in excitement

The first paycheck, and the last,
Clapped together for beauty and joy,
Astonishment and gratitude,
Folded tight in the urgency of prayer,
And lifted skyward in awe
At a simple rise of the morning sun.
In the long silence of my pondering,
She looks at her own hands, and asks
"Will mine look like that when I get old?"
"If you're lucky," I tell her.
She looks back at me as if I'm crazy,
Then bounces off the couch to go play.

Family Genes

As far back as I can remember,
I romped with dogs, admired frogs,
Rescued spiders from a crushing death,
Stroked the bellies of horned toads,
Feeling their skin as smooth as beads.
I rescued bees from the swimming pool
Even though I knew they'd sting,
Wheedled a horse by junior high,
And made excuses for my parrot
Every single time he'd bite me.
I had extravagant love
For all the animal world
From the day I was born.

Who knows from which family genes
These passions spring?
Somewhere way back in time
I thought we might have shepherds
Or zookeepers or sheep-doting weavers,
Or cheesemakers who adored their cows.
Tracing the lines back my brother found
A few of these. Also laborers,
And one more discovery: Killer.

I imagine this man, my relation,
Standing in his rough apron
With a razor sharp knife,
Preparing to slice the line
Between being and meat,
Blood on his hands,
Expressing his genes
By killing animals.

How do our distant ancestors
Give us genetic direction anyway?
Maybe like this:
Some genes press us forward
To repeat and repeat and repeat their traits.
Others beg us to redeem them.

Close Kin

I talk to most everything these days:
The ginkgo tree, the frying pan,
Our honeysuckle-burdened wooden fence,
The wobbly flagstones, the ferns,
Even the earth in the northeast corner
Of the front yard. My tongue waggles on
With words of encouragement, questions,
Expressions of thanks. Plant, metal,
Wood, stone, mud. Who knew
These were my close kin?
By some molecular sleight of hand,
I turned out to be human.
They seem to tolerate my babble,
Patiently waiting for the day
When I speak their language,
When I'm a rock or pond or tree.

Under the Influence

I am old and under the influence
Of my aging body and brain,
But no one really knows just what
That means. Inside my elder head
My hippocampus may still be
Churning out neurons as numerous
As in a teenybopper's bobbing noggin.
At least that's what a recent study says.
I like to think of my been-there-done-that
Brain frolicking away like a young filly,
Bucking, jumping, and sparking up
Fresh nerve cells amongst the old,
And that my memories and cognition,
My many-hued emotions and intuition,
My mistakes and regrets and lessons,
My assumptions and hard-won wisdom
Teach my new neurons to prance
Amidst swelling shadows
And fields of thinning grass,
And that when my time is spent,
They carry me with ease
And strong synaptic grace
Up and over my final fence.

Old Beds

I wonder about old beds
And what happened in them,
How they may have wobbled
With kids bouncing up and down,
How they must have creaked
With lovers swelling and spooning.
The soft, firm, lumpy, or unyielding,
The brassbound, canopied, or boxed in,
Those musty, dusty faithful witnesses
To love and sickness, DNA and dreams
Of sleepers, the tossers-and-turners,
The deep breathers, the damned snorers,
The frolickers, the wearily troubled,
That little nest for despair to curl up in,
And for hope to grow,
Just like old garden beds, nurturers
Of darkness, earthworms, and seeds,
Roses, geraniums, dahlias, fantasies,
Holders of memories, the sharp shovels,
Piercing trowels, bumper crops, bad seasons,
The awed delight of a little girl
Finding her first strawberry there.
How those old beds hold tears too,
And, finally, in their depths, everything.

Derelict

Half of her shingles flew with the last flock
Of pigeons wheeling high in a freshening breeze.
Proud windows no longer rouged by cherry red
Curtains gone; wide-open frames welcome the wind.

The porch slants in a crooked jaunty smile
Of wry humor. Her stairs step out with blackberries
Swelling in a thick crowd of loitering suitors
Competing with cow parsnip and morning glory vines.

In her prime, baubled walls and tidy carpeted rooms
Framed a haughty family intent on the display
Of wealth, fine taste, first class perfection all the way.
Her appearance was never quite enough to please.

Poked, primed, posed, photographed, redone,
Until the wealth ran out, contents carted away.
She breathed in alarm, and then relief,
Though she wept for the children.

Her once exclusive address has sprung open wide
To flocks of birds, slithers of snakes, and skittering mice,
Peripatetic drifters find kind shelter in her sagging arms,
Red tailed hawks perch daily on her splintered ridgeline.

Like a fragile old woman, she sits in her favorite spot,
Unkempt, wispy hair framing a weathered face.
Her shaking hands hold bread from her little bag.
She offers her final crumbs to the wild doves.

The Whole Entourage

As recompense for ignorance
God gave us sense
To let the world in.

Our portals rattle endlessly
With the world's unceasing traffic
Rushing in and rambling out,
Then striding in again,
Like the whole entourage of creation
Cartwheeling by for our consideration.

We breathe in what's around us—
Balsam's balm and fresh rain at dawn
Or pepper that pricks to a sneeze,
Or the calm fragrance of salt,
Or that trace of a skunk's perfume
Left to waft on a willful breeze.

Our blue, or brown, or green-flecked
Fields of vision fill with wonders
Of summers rising yellow, or the grey
Of slick slate in the fog, or the iridescent
Hint of hummingbirds,
Or a speckled fawn.

Unremitting, the world's waves roll
Through convoluted canals, breaking
On our shores in Mozart or mayhem,
Or a brass band of birdsong, with a virtuoso flicker
Drumming the chimney like nobody's business,
While our tympana vibrate wildly with the beat.

And, oh, the world that caresses the skin
Like a lover, who thrusts an urgent touch,
Or unfolds a slow cascade of luscious silk
Sliding in on tenderness and finishing in fire,
Or warm soil on our hands and seeds in our pockets,
Or the brush of a wild wind rushing in from a surging sea.

We lap up life like the perpetually starved
Creatures that we are, and make it ours—
The peach dripping with the juice of summer,
Fresh sharp bite of basil, or a blessing of butter,
Or raspberry swirls lacing creamy custard
Caught on the cusp of a tongue.

And then all sense stops.
Ignorance becomes knowing.
The whole entourage moves on,
Fleet as a flock of passerines,
Flying away, singing.

Wonder

I always wonder
What leaves feel
When they unfurl,
Or when they twirl
Free of a branch.

I wonder about eggs,
Nested and quiet,
When sharp beaks
Break them to shattering.

I wonder about swans
Scribing the sky goodbye
And flying in migration
To somewhere way beyond.

I wonder how the first,
Or final, breath feels.
Does the soul steel
Against a dark unknown
Or open like a flower?

Publication Attributions

Thanks to the editors of the following publications in which some of these poems have previously appeared (some in slightly different form):

These Fragile Lilacs: "Aubade to Dawn," "Stars," "Tending Trees"

Clover, a Literary Rag: "Fish Pond," "Cow and Ganges," "Buddha Belly," "Doors of the Moon," "Hands"

Sue C. Boynton Winning Poems Anthology, 2013: "Great Blue"

The Plum Tree Tavern: "Wild Water"

The Bellingham Herald: "A Blessing for Cantankerous Couples," "Garden Love"

Last Call: Anthology of Beer, Wine, and Spirits Poetry, World Enough Writers Press, 2018: "Old Wine, For My Husband"

Bindweed: "Wu Tong Triolet"

Cirque: A Literary Journal for the North Pacific Rim: "The Old Women," "My Husband's Map"

Front Porch Review: "Close Kin"

Acknowledgements

I'm ever-grateful to my husband for his creativity, discernment, and support of my writing in all its forms, foibles, and drafts. And for his generosity in sharing his exquisite line drawings that float gracefully through the pages of this book.

Bushels of thanks to the accomplished members of my monthly poetry group, *Submit!* Susan Chase-Foster and Judy Kleinberg, you inspire me with your insights, knowledge, and skill. I admire your work and am blessed by your encouragement.

Utmost appreciation goes to Red Wheelbarrow Writers, and to Laura Kalpakian and Cami Ostman for your unfailing dedication in fostering such a vibrant community of writers. Also thanks to the many groups that encourage and celebrate writers, including Speakeasy, Chuckanut Sandstone Poetry Theater, the late, great *Clover, A Literary Rag*, and, last but not least, the independent bookstore par excellence, Village Books.

Thanks to my writing groups Talespinners and Wranglers, and to Rody Rowe and Joe Nolting, talented poets, advisors, and friends. To my brother and his family, gratitude for your ever-present support. And thanks to my chosen sisters Janet, Kim, Marilyn, Mary, and Nancy, you steady my boat and urge me forward.

Bouquets of gratitude to my publisher, Jes Stone of Penchant Press International, whose heart for my poetry lead her to bring it forth in the form of a book. Your encouragement, know-how, willingness to experiment, and confidence in the project kept me going.

Victoria Doerper

Victoria Doerper writes poetry and creative nonfiction from her cottage near the shore of the Salish Sea. Inspired by nature and the small things of this world, her poems examine love, loss, and wonder. Her work appears in several literary publications, including *Cirque*, *Clover*, *Front Porch Review*, and *The Plum Tree Tavern* as well as in *Orion* Magazine.

John Doerper

John Doerper is an artist whose work has appeared in juried shows. He's also an author of award-winning books about food, wine, and travel. The burgeoning garden he created in the yard of the cottage he and Victoria share inspires many of his drawings.